the brief guide

to an

extraordinary
college
experience

*simple strategies to help you
excel at college....and life!!!*

dr. david f. spigelman

table of contents

acknowledgements

This guide was written to give ideas to current and future college students that will help them get more out of their college experience. Before writing this book, I interviewed some of my brightest and most "extraordinary" college students at the University of Miami, where I am a lecturer in economics and finance. The quotes included herein were inspired by many of their ideas and are meant to stimulate thought in the reader; these are not the exact quotes of the students interviewed---in some cases, the quotes were created mainly by me. Their names have been changed and I am solely responsible for the content of this book.

The "Extraordinary College Experience Student Advisory Council" included Chris Seifel, Kiran Sethi, Michael Gotterer, Kiara Green, Melissa Butler, Stephanie Velasco, Andrew Fernandez, Lara Ryan, Julia Cerullo, and Sophie Raymond.

before we get started

A tremendous amount has been written about getting into college. There are books on the admissions process, books to help you study for SATs, books to help you write a spectacular, attention-grabbing essay, and so on and so forth. But what are you going to do once you are there? Little time and attention has been devoted to this topic.

How you perform, what you do during that time, and what you learn over the course of four years will to a large extent determine how successful you will be in later years. This book will give you many ideas and insights into how to make the experience in college more productive, in order to give you the best chance for success in college, and more importantly, for the rest of your life!

My purpose in writing this book is to help college students improve their chance for success in college, but really it goes beyond that. [Setting up the patterns and methods for a productive college experience will also set the patterns and methods for a productive and successful life.]

This book aims to help you do better in college, but it also aims to make college more meaningful, fulfilling and enjoyable for you as well. Being an outstanding college student does not mean that you have to be a grind who never thinks about anything but grades.

It is true that if you are hoping to practice medicine, you will have to get very good grades in order to have a chance to be accepted to medical school. On the other hand, there are skills that may help one become a successful businessperson, for example, that may not be taught in class. How you spend your time during your college years should be reflective of what you plan to do after college, at least to the extent that you have some idea of what you want to do after college. If you do, there are activities that you can participate in during your college years that will help you to be successful in later years. If you don't know what you want to do later, there are activities that you can participate in that will help you make that choice, and again, could provide skills and experience that will be useful later.

The spirit of this book is aimed at empowering the college student to make better and more informed choices as to how to use their time during the college years. Time will be a scarce and precious commodity. Thinking a little bit upfront about how you approach the college experience and devising personal strategies for succeeding at college will pay tremendous dividends for the rest of your life.

1. be prepared

College is not going to be like high school. Maybe you were one of the better students at your high school and you will be attending Cornell. Guess what, the average student will be better than the average student in your Calc AB class in high school. Check your ego at the door. You can strive to be *extraordinary*, but you may not be the *best* in everything anymore.

Some students will find college to be a bit of a shock at first. The assignments seem endless and the work load may seem overwhelming. You may have to accept a feeling of sort of "swimming in it" for a while.

It didn't happen to me when I went to college. (I went to the University of Illinois at Urbana-Champaign.) But when I got to Stanford, where I pursued and earned my master's and doctoral degrees in economics, boy did I get hit with it. There are a lot of smart people out there. Don't let them *don't let others intimidate you b/c you have a goal to accomplish but you can still learn from them.*

intimidate you. You will find your voice with time.

Maybe you will hit the ground running when you get to college and everything will be a breeze. If so, more power to you. But if not, remember that you are not alone. You may have feelings of homesickness, anxiety, stress, etc. You'll probably feel better if you remind yourself to be patient. Freshman year, especially the first semester, is going to be an adjustment process. If everything doesn't fall into place immediately, don't panic. Take a deep breath and remind yourself that this is natural for many people. If you give yourself some time, you will find that you will make the adjustment. Many, if not most people, eventually find that the college years were among their most pleasurable. But at first, the process of change can be disorienting for many. (If you become depressed or feel unable to cope with college life, you should seek counseling. Most schools have counselors available. Don't be afraid to ask for help.)

It is important to make time for stress-relieving activities in college. Try to get to the gym on a regular basis, or make time to run or ride your bike. A big part of becoming an extraordinary college student is to set patterns that you can live with. You are more likely to be productive and successful in college if you are healthy, both mentally and physically.

· eat right
· exercise
· go to bed early when you can.

Most students will be academically prepared for college. If you were accepted to a competitive university, you were accepted for a reason and at least the admissions staff believes you to be ready for college. On the other hand, if you didn't study math in your last year of high school, it may be worthwhile to tune up your math skills before you arrive on campus. Reviewing your old textbooks or taking a short online course can help to accomplish this. If you are aware of any other deficiencies in your academic preparation for college, you should take steps to correct those deficiencies before starting college.

It is also important to prepare mentally for your arrival on campus. Get the things out of your system you need to do out before you arrive on campus. If you always wanted to run a marathon, train for it and do it before starting college. You might not have the time to train adequately once you are ensconced in college life. Although I am going to encourage you to aim high in this book, you don't want to bite off more than you can chew and lose focus on your principal goals for the college experience.

· Set goals
· mission statement

"You'll never have a reason to want to do your best if you don't have goals that require you to challenge yourself."   Sabrina, a sophomore

"Create a mission statement for yourself. Know it, write it down, put it up on your wall. You won't lose motivation, if you see this every day."   Josh, a junior

2. aim high

Set goals for yourself. Set goals for your GPA (grade point average). Set social goals. Set goals to join organizations. Set goals for academic distinctions. Set any other goals you can think of.

goals start
the baby steps
of the long
journey

You may not reach all of your goals. But setting goals can lead you to try to do more and will generally lead to greater achievement. You don't know if you can achieve anything until you try and you'll try harder if you have a goal or goals in mind.

It is a good idea to map out a plan for your four years. What do you think could be a reasonable goal for a GPA? Now add a few points and aim for that. Push yourself a little. You could be pleasantly surprised.

Try to design a plan that maps out when you expect to choose a major. Give yourself an idea of how many and what types of campus activities you want to be involved with. In many types of future endeavors---business for example---leadership skills are important. How are you going to become a future leader if you're not involved during your college years? Set yourself a plan for achieving leadership roles within organizations that you can get involved with.

Social goals are important too. How many friends can you make? Introduce yourself to the people sitting next to you in class. Later you may want to form a study group with your neighbors in class or even get a date for Saturday night. Don't be shy. Leave that back in high school, if that's the way you were.

Do you want to join a fraternity or sorority? Discuss the pros and cons with your friends. Sign up for rush if you think you might have an interest and/or try to talk with upperclassmen who have experienced Greek life. The fraternity/sorority system is not for everyone, but for some it creates a network of friends that can last a lifetime. Greeks also get involved in organizing activities like fundraisers and campus events that can build organizational and leadership skills for individuals that get involved.

Find out what it takes to get elected to honor societies and honors programs on campus. Is it realistic to aim for those goals? Why not give it a shot?

make a list
the first week
w/ office hrs.
numbers & emails ☺ →

"Professors are the best people to give you 'expert advice' on your career...rather than your friends, your parents or the internet."   Meryl, a junior

3. befriend thy professor

This is probably the easiest and best advice I can give to any college student: "Go and see your professor during office hours." If you can't see your professor during his/her regularly scheduled office hours, many professors will allow students to make appointments to see them. Go see your professors!!!

As a lecturer in economics and finance at the University of Miami, I know that only a small minority of my students will come and see me during office hours. Moreover, most of those students will arrive a day or two prior to the midterm or final, when my office is finally full of students looking to get a leg up on the exam. This is okay, but it's even better to visit your professors when they aren't so busy earlier in the term or just after midterms.

There are at least four reasons why I can tell you that it is a great strategy to go and visit your professors:

1) They have a chance to get to know who you are. Someday, you may need a recommendation for law

bonus –
· recommendations

school or a summer job. They are more likely to write you a good recommendation if they know who you are. Professors may have lots of students. They have a better chance of remembering you if they see you outside of class. You have a better chance of getting a great recommendation from someone who knows you, relative to someone who just thinks of you as a name and a grade.

2) You may get insight for the tests. You can ask your professor about the homework problems you are having

trouble with or about the material that is likely to be on the upcoming test. Many students use outside tutors to help with their studies. Who is going to be a better tutor: the professor giving the test or a hired hand? The answer, obviously, is the professor. Some professors will not make themselves easily accessible. If this is the case, at least you tried. But many professors, myself included, have a hard time saying no to students, and in fact like to help *interested* students. Showing up in their office demonstrates motivation and interest.

3) Whether they admit or not, when they know you and they know you are trying, they may be more inclined to give you a better grade. Effort is important to many professors. By visiting during office hours, you are demonstrating that you are trying to succeed in their class. Believe it or not, professors are human beings.

They tend to be more sympathetic to students that they believe are trying hard to succeed in their course and are putting forth the effort.

4) When you visit professors outside of class, they may offer other useful insights to you. Professors are usually glad to help students who need guidance on how to choose a major, what types of summer jobs are likely to be beneficial to a student, career planning issues, and on and on. Professors are usually pretty smart people who may be able to act as a mentor to you and give you guidance on a host of issues. You'll never know until you reach out to them. The best place to start is office hours!

Not all professors are open to students, but you don't know which professors will be open and forthcoming until you make the effort to see them. Some professors will be very open and like to help students. Part of the benefit of being a professor is the satisfaction of seeing your students grow and achieve academic, social, business or any other form of success. To some professors, students can almost be like their children and they view their students as a reflection of them. They want their students to succeed in life and will make efforts to help them be successful.

I know I feel this way as a professor. I've had students get accepted into prestigious graduate programs and I feel good about the role that I've played in helping that student reach his or her maximum potential. By interacting and even befriending your professor, you're giving that professor a chance to help you, and many professors will seize the opportunity to be a help.

Some professors will go even further in reaching out to students. Professors are not generally qualified to be psychologists, but if there is a personal problem that has kept you from coming to class or is interfering with your studies, it may be worth discussing the situation with your professor. They may help you make up for missed class time with additional help, if they know about your situation.

Students with learning differences should also try to meet with professors. Let them know what they can do to help make your learning experience better. Most of the time, professors will be sympathetic and will make every effort to help each student reach his or her potential.

"I used to be afraid to speak in class, but now I try to raise my hand and participate; it's helped me conquer my fear of public speaking -- the more I participate, the less afraid I become."
David, a senior

4. speak up, stand out

Another easy piece of advice to college students: "sit in the front row and raise your hand from time to time."

Many students sit in the back of the room and even fall asleep when they come to class. Don't be one of those! Don't come to class when you're falling asleep, it's an insult to the professor. Grab a cup of coffee or do what you need to do to wake up.

Get engaged in the class. It will be more interesting and you'll remember things better for the test. Professors appreciate students who contribute to the class discussion and/or ask interesting questions. There is no such thing as a dumb question to a good professor and professors would rather teach to an engaged and interactive class.

You will get noticed by asking good questions and participating in class discussions. Even better, ask a question before or after class. That demonstrates to the professor that you are stimulated by the class material and are not just passively attending class because you have to be there.

Just like visiting the professor outside of class, speaking up and participating in class makes it more likely that the professor will remember your name and remember you. He or she may even be more positively predisposed toward you when it comes time to assigning grades. Many professors will even give credit for class participation and attendance. Why not get those brownie points????

"Join the honors society/honors college. Take challenging courses, but pick you subjects WISELY! ... and pick your professors even more WISELY!!! Don't just aim for the grade you need, aim to be the best in class."
Sophie, a sophomore

5. upgrade to first class

Many colleges and universities offer honors programs to certain undergraduates. Usually there is a grade point average criterion, but there may also be an applications process or required recommendations, etc. These honors programs can be structured in a variety of ways. Sometimes there is an honors program for a specific major such as "Honors Biology" or sometimes it is a broader approach. Find out what it takes to get into the honors program at your institution.

← Look into?

Honors programs are a way of standing out from the crowd. You may be able to interact more frequently with professors and you may also get smaller class sizes in honors courses. It will eventually look good on your resume to have participated in honors courses and you will likely get to know your professors better.

Many times you will get access to more challenging curricula and there may be opportunities to do advanced research or help professors with their own research.

If you are a student at a public institution or less competitive university, honors programs are a way of upgrading your brand, generally without paying additional fees for the privilege. For example, the honors program at the University of Florida entails no additional fees, and the cost of tuition for in-state residents at the University of Florida is a fraction of that paid at Ivy League schools. For many students, an honors program is a discounted way to earn a prestigious degree.

Often universities confer distinction at graduation time for having participated in the honors program or sometimes for writing undergraduate theses. I was able to get "distinction in economics" attached to my B.A. degree at the University of Illinois for a senior thesis that I wrote on the "Impact of American Aid on Agriculture in the Andean Countries of Latin America" when I was an undergraduate at the University of Illinois. (I also used this as an excuse to travel to Peru for field research with a professor who had been a visiting professor at my school. That was another great experience for me during my college years.)

Also, most universities confer distinction for finishing in certain percentiles of your class when you complete your degree: *summa cum laude*, *magna cum laude*, and *cum laude*, with *summa cum laude* being the highest distinction.

"Freshman year, I didn't get to the gym at all. I put on 7 pounds. Since then I found that both my grades and my looks improved when I made it a priority to get to the gym three days a week; it relieves stress and helps me focus when I am studying." Kayla, a senior

6. get your priorities straight

Different people will have different types of study habits that will work for them. Some people like to be around others while they're studying, whereas others need to isolate themselves in a soundproof booth. Most universities offer a variety of locations where students can study, including libraries, classrooms, student unions, dorm rooms, etc. At many universities, going higher in the library means you're more serious about studying and the library gets quieter as you rise in altitude.

You will have to figure out what works for you. If you're spending hours at the library, but not getting anything done, you probably need to rethink your study strategy.

Most solid students won't procrastinate until the night before the exam to do their studying. It is best to keep up with the assigned readings as you move through the course and not try to cram it in at the end immediately before the exam. I call this binge and purge learning; bulimics don't get much nutrition from this process and neither do students who try to cram it in at the end. The goal of your education is mainly to improve your ability to think and analyze problems. Unfortunately, most of us don't remember everything we learn. I really believe that students who focus on building up their critical thinking and reasoning ability won't have to cram as much before tests and will rely on their reasoning ability, written communication skills and logic to achieve higher test scores. Memorizing as much as possible and writing everything you know on the exam is generally not a strong strategy for college test-taking and definitely not a strong strategy for getting the most benefit from your college experience.

If you keep up with the class, you will have an easier time contributing to the in-class discussions and when you go to the professor's office hours, he/she will recognize that you have put effort into the class and thus will generally respond more favorably to your questions. One of my pet peeves as a professor is the student who doesn't come to class, but shows up in office hours the day or two before the exam, hoping for a crash course that will get him/her through the exam with a passing grade. I myself will not provide tutoring for students who demonstrate that they have not been putting any effort into the class.

We will see in later chapters, that what you do outside of the classroom may be as important to your college experience – and getting the most out of college – as your classroom and study activities. It is important to organize your time wisely, beyond just studying all the time. You will have to decide what has the most meaning for you and what can help you to have the most productive college experience; it is not only about getting a high GPA. Other experiences that you participate in while at college can be very important to your development as an individual and can help you gain skills and confidence that may be important to your future success -- and even happiness -- in life.

"I used to get frustrated when I got poor grades on essay-type exam questions; I started to improve when I made more of an effort to think about what the professor was looking for in the question and trying to make logical arguments backed up with evidence from the text or course material." Mia, a senior

7. read the question

Test-taking is probably the most stressful part of the college experience for many college students. Sending yourself positive messages and trying to reduce the stress one places on oneself are some techniques that can be used that might help you perform better on tests. Remember, it is good to get good grades, but once you get out of the academic environment, there is a lot more that goes into making a successful life than just your grade point average. Try to increase your emphasis on learning for the sake of learning. Prepare yourself as well as you can, and tell yourself that as long as you've given it your best effort, you are going to be willing to accept the grade you receive.

As a teacher, I am willing to admit that I have some pet peeves. One of the biggest is that I really don't like getting exams back from a student that writes everything he or she knows about a topic. *Answer the question!!!!* Be concise and to the point. If it is a verbal question, ask yourself what it is that the professor looking for. Take time to read and

understand the question. If you have questions about the question, ask the professor! He/she will generally be willing to answer questions that clarify what he or she is looking for.

Reread your test and make sure that you have answered all aspects of the test question. If it is a verbal analysis, ask yourself if your answer is logical and concise. Does the answer represent your best thinking and is it to the point? Don't engage in binge and purge learning. Be thoughtful in your answers to the questions on exams. Make a reasoned argument where applicable. Remember, it is quality and not quantity that matters to most professors.

"I get a lot out of participating in service projects; it's a chance to develop leadership, organizational and communication skills and I feel great giving back." Ellie, a freshman

8. do the right thing

To be extraordinary, you've got to be ethical also. Guard your reputation for personal integrity. It's the most valuable thing you have.

Unfortunately, it's become so ordinary to be a cheater. There has always been cheating on college campuses and, unfortunately, there will probably always be cheating. But because other people are doing something, it doesn't mean that you have to do it.

Suppose your professor assigns a take-home exam and you find out that others are working together despite the professor having made it clear that he/she expects independent work. Does this justify teaming up with a smart classmate to improve your prospects for an A?

The answer is a resounding NOOOOOO!!! It may be cliché, but cheating on an exam is cheating against yourself, not for yourself. Your main goal in college should be to improve yourself as a human being. People have different motives for attending college, but for most people a primary goal is to get a good job after college and to get on the path to an interesting and rewarding life. Cheating could end all of that in a heartbeat. Most schools will consider throwing you out of school if you are caught cheating. Expulsion would be like a scarlet A that would follow you around the rest of your life.

Once you are out of college, you probably won't be taking exams that frequently anymore. If you cheat your way through college, what are you going to do when you're at work? Plagiarize, rely on your colleagues, phone mom for advice? College should help you forge the skills that will help you later in the working environment. It's not going to help you if you have to cheat your way through. The long-term payoff to cheating is negative and, if you are caught, you can easily ruin your chances for success almost entirely.

Instead, the extraordinary college student should take every opportunity to make a commitment to the "community", whether it be the college community, the local community, the nation or even the global community. Community service may help you gain leadership skills and will look good on your resume. In addition, probably the greatest benefit will be the psychic benefit you get from feeling that you're making a contribution.

I can tell you that one of the greatest benefits of being a teacher is the feeling that you're helping at least some kids reach their greatest potential. Give yourself the opportunity to feel good about yourself by making a contribution to the community in some way, even while you're a busy college student. If you do, you will reap many rewards, I can assure you.

"A lot of the information that you'll find useful in determining your career path is found on your own time by your own effort. I found out a lot about my interests through online research. Janie, a junior

"Students bar themselves from success when they see their failures as dead-ends. To be successful, we have to change the way we think – we must think of our failures as challenges to prove ourselves – how quickly we can recover and what we can learn from our mistakes – not only academically, but in our personal lives." Katie, a sophomore

9. think outside the box ....and the <u>classroom!</u>

College is about more than just accumulating a strong GPA. It is true that if your goal is to attend medical school or a prestigious law school, you will most likely need to achieve a high GPA. However, even medical schools and law schools will look at your complete range of activities as an undergraduate and are looking for certain qualities, depth of experience, leadership skills and other attributes when considering your application for admission.

I spent most of my career in business and I know that when I looked to hire individuals, I would look for lots of factors beside just the strength of their undergraduate institution and GPA when considering their job applications. In business, attributes like leadership skills, ability to take initiative, presentation skills, reliability and ethics, personality, teamwork and a host of other factors are important in predicting business success. To me, the outside activities of a college student were generally equal in importance to the prestige of his/her undergraduate degree and overall GPA.

Please don't plan to spend your entire four years at college buried at the library every night until 3:00 am. Join campus groups that arouse your curiosity or interest. If you like sports, join a club or play intramural sports if you're not able to make the varsity team. Get involved with campus political groups or the school newspaper. In particular, it is worth getting involved in activities that can lead to the opportunity to demonstrate leadership skills. Many graduate programs and future employers will look particularly favorably on candidates that are demonstrated leaders through their college activities.

If an organization does not exist that you'd like to participate in, start it up yourself!! Demonstrating a willingness to take initiative will be extremely attractive to future employers and/or graduate programs.

When I was an undergraduate, I became the president of my dorm and participated in an organization known as the "Council of Presidents" which provided student input into the residence policies of the University of Illinois. I also helped to create a Judicial Board for my dorm to resolve disputes between students/residents as well as disciplinary issues and helped to produce dorm events like concerts and lectures and wrote record reviews for the school newspaper. All of these activities gave me great experiences, allowed me to develop leadership skills and helped me to evolve from a relatively shy, less secure individual into a more self-confident, student leader.

You will never know what your true potential as an individual can be unless you challenge yourself. Getting involved while you are at college is a great place to start.

Another aspect of thinking outside the classroom which I believe is extremely important is to challenge yourself to become more aware of the world around you. College is a great opportunity to explore activities, events, and subject matter that may be somewhat foreign and unknown to you. Go to that lecture on Zen philosophy or listen to a speaker talk about his experiences hiking through Nepal. Discuss current events with your classmates and/or dorm friends. Check out dance, theater and other performances of student groups. You'll most likely never have the variety of new opportunities or experiences so easily accessible as while you are a college student. Try it, you'll like it!!!

I also think it is imperative for college students to keep themselves informed about current events. In college, you are beginning to create patterns that you will likely follow, at least to some extent, for the rest of your life. It is important for individuals to be informed in modern society. Access to information has never been as easy as it is now. Make sure you know what's going on, whether you get your information from the newspaper, online news sources, blogs, television, radio, etc. You have a great opportunity while a college student to discuss ideas with your peers. This is where a lot of great learning takes place. Seize the day and form your own opinions. Explore the world of ideas and allow yourself to experience the pleasure of informed debate.

Independent research during your later years in college can also be a great way to explore topics that interest you and to get a different type of learning experience. Maybe you are interested in Victorian literature or Greek philosophy and want to explore it in greater detail.

If you are thinking of going on for a PhD, you may want to practice doing independent research and this is a great way of getting that practice. You'll get a chance to see if you like to produce research, which is what most academics have to focus on.

"I like to challenge myself to see how much I can achieve, not only in the classroom but outside   the classroom as well. I have many interests and   I don't think college should stop me from pursuing any of my passions."
Joe, a junior

10.do more

College is a time to experiment. Never again will you have so many opportunities to have so many different experiences. *Carpe diem---seize the day!!*

Maybe you've always wanted to learn to sail—join the sailing club. You love sports but can't make the NCAA Division I team? Try intramurals. Attend a lecture by a Nobel laureate in economics, join a folk dancing club, establish a charity or produce a fundraiser, get involved in a political campaign, write for the student newspaper, run for class president. DO SOMETHING!! In fact, do MORE than something. Get involved.

In college, you are beginning to set patterns that you may follow the rest of your life. Do you aspire to be a grind that only does one thing the rest of your life? Are you going to plant yourself in front of the TV at every opportunity. If so, I'd probably prefer not to meet you.

Set the pattern of trying to keep in shape. Do something active a few times a week. Set the pattern of being involved in your community. Can you manage a few hours a week for a community service activity? When I was in college, I tutored less-advantaged high school kids. I remember really enjoying working with the kids and feeling good about helping them aspire to greater achievements. Maybe that's why I've come back to teaching later in my career. It's so rewarding to help students reach their potential and to shake them out of their complacency.

Set the pattern of being a leader. Run for a political office (president of your dorm or your class, local council person, etc.) or organize a new club. When I was a business person looking to hire someone, I always scanned their resume to see what types of leadership positions they had attained or where they had shown initiative in their background. I don't think I would have hired anyone who was not able to show that they were willing and able to take initiative. You can gain these types of experiences in college by being involved. If an organization doesn't exist that you would like to become involved with, start it yourself!!! This is a great way of showing that you can take initiative and begin to work on your leadership skills. Many future employers will look for these attributes.

"I always try to talk to my professors during office hours or outside of class. I find they appreciate an interested student and often give me interesting advice. I know that I'll eventually need recommendations for law school, and I want there to be professors who know me and can say something personal that will make my recommendation letters stand out." Jason, a junior

11. network, network, network

You may not realize that the friendships and social engagements you form in college are probably going to turn into your most important career-related network for the rest of your life. When you get to the point of looking for jobs, you will often find that you usually end up landing a job through a series of associations. In other words, you will often be referred to a job through a "friend of a friend." Thus, it is useful to make friends and to keep in contact with those friends over time. You get a near-term benefit from having a lot of friends and you will get a long-term benefit as well. You may find that your college friends are your best referral network when looking for work or to change jobs throughout your life.

Not only should friends become part of your network, but professors and almost everybody else you come into contact with along the way. This is another reason why it is useful to develop relationships with professors. They may have ideas and contacts for you when you begin to search for jobs.

"In preparation to be successful in our future, one of our greatest downfalls is losing sight of the main point of college -- to let ourselves leave our comfort zone and to enjoy new experiences. We forget that college is also about taking joy in learning -- about immersing ourselves in topics and studies that interest us." Kirsten, a sophomore

12. inhabit the moment

When I was in high school, there was a popular book with the title "Be Here Now," which had something to do with eastern religion. I'm not sure I can recommend the book, but I love the title. Be "in the moment"---it only comes around once in your life. Relish the privilege of being able to focus on studying and learning. Most likely, you will never have the opportunity to focus solely on learning at any future point in your life. You may have the opportunity to go to some type of graduate school or take continuing education programs later in life, but you will never have the opportunity to take the diversity of courses and have the diversity of experiences that you can have as an undergraduate.

Many college students, unfortunately, do not pay attention to current events or what is going on in the world around them. This is a terrible mistake!! Part of being an educated person is being aware of and involved with the activities in the broader community and the world at large. It is so easy to gain access to information since the advent of the technology and internet revolution. Take the time each day to see what is going on in the world.

Take advantage of class time when you are in class. When you are in class, really be in class! Participate in the class discussions and enjoy the experience. A positive attitude can go a long way to making the material seem more interesting and relevant to your life. Don't walk through life half asleep. *Carpe diem.* Seize the day!!!

"Always, always enjoy yourself, or else the stress will wear you out, and you'll end up defining your college experience as a series of stresses to be endured. You have to learn time management and leave time to have a good time in between all the other million things on your 'to do' list. But don't party the night before your midterms. That might not be wise!"   Isabelle, a senior

13. leave time to party

You don't have to be a grind who never has a good time to be an extraordinary college student. Socializing and partying with other students is definitely part of the college experience. Work partying into your schedule just like everything else.

The main point is to not overdo it. Partying shouldn't start until classes are finished. Friday afternoon classes should not be "blown off" on a regular basis. This is disrespectful to the professor. If you are not going to attend Friday afternoon classes, try to arrange your schedule so that you don't have to cut class to join the party.

Being responsible and staying out of trouble should also be key objectives of the extraordinary college student. Participating in illicit activities and making bad choices when intoxicated can lead to life-changing events and almost always for the worse. Leaving time to party does not mean "leaving time to be irresponsible and stupid." Sorry to lecture here, but many college students allow themselves to get swept along with the crowd. Extraordinary college students should be more discerning. You can have a good time without getting to the point where you get involved with activities or find yourself in situations that you may come to regret.

"I want to start my own business someday; I'm trying to get as much practice as possible at being entrepreneurial in ways that don't involve a financial outlay."
Jacob, a sophomore

14. jumpstart the rest of your life

A lot of students still don't know "what they want to be when they grow up" when they reach college. This is okay. You don't have to know what you want to be at this point to be successful in life. But if you don't know what you want to do for life, use your time in college to acquire information and experience to help you make better choices.

You can spend the first year or two of college shopping for a major. Take courses in subjects that you are interested in and see what you like. Talk to your professors and see what advice they have for you. How does your aptitude match up with the subjects that you are interested in? You are probably not going to be a nuclear physicist if you aren't good in math.

Try to make some connection between your interests and a possible career direction. If you are unsure, explore internships, independent study programs, course work or jobs that can help you gain valuable experience to be able to make more informed choices.

Summer jobs and internships can often give you valuable experience that may even help you get into graduate programs later as well as giving you insight into what a potential career choice may be like.

You do have to be realistic about the decisions you make. If you are a music major and wish to pursue a career in performance, you have to be realistic as to whether you have the talent to be able to earn a living in this fashion. Again, talking to professors and getting feedback should help you make a more informed decision.

Ideas to explore possible future career directions in:

<u>Medicine</u> -- internships with local hospitals and doctors, independent research projects into scientific/medical topics, volunteer programs at local hospitals.

<u>Business/entrepreneurship</u> -- try to start your own web-related business or run a fundraiser on campus. Firms love to see individuals that take initiative and demonstrate leadership capability. Almost anything you do to make a profit or raise funds for charity can be seen as a desirable experience. Start a new club or a tutoring program for high school students in the inner city. Produce a rock concert or concert series in your dorm.

Internships are also useful here if you have a particular area of interest like finance or marketing. Try to work with firms that you might want to be hired by after college.

<u>Law</u> -- see if you can intern for a local attorney or get involved with a law professor's "justice project" or other types of pro bono work.

Resources for Finding Summer Internships:

www.campuscareercenter.com – a clearinghouse for entry level jobs and summer internships where you can post resumes and search listings.

www.college.monster.com – special resources for college students, including internship search.

afterword

I hope you have enjoyed this brief book and it has given you some ideas as to how you can better capitalize on your college experience. Make college work for you in your own way. Think about what your objectives are for college and try to plan out a strategy for reaching your objectives. College is much more than an opportunity to establish a grade point average. Make sure you see the big picture when it comes to designing your college experience and don't just let it wash over you like a big wave. Take control of your own life and try to get the most out the experience. After all who wants to be just ordinary?